How to Improve Your Relationship With Your Mom

Have the relationship with your Mother that you've always wanted

By Jean Young

EXPERIENCE
EVERYTHING
PUBLISHING

Disclaimer

This document is geared towards providing exact and reliable information in regards to the topic and issue covered. The publication is sold with the idea that the publisher is not required to render accounting, officially permitted, or otherwise, qualified services. If advice is necessary, legal or professional, a practiced individual in the profession should be ordered.

- From a Declaration of Principles which was accepted and approved equally by a Committee of the American Bar Association and a Committee of Publishers and Associations:

The information herein is offered for informational purposes solely, and is universal as so. The presentation of the information is without contract or any type of guarantee assurance.

The trademarks that are used are without any consent, and the publication of the trademark is without permission or backing by the trademark owner. All trademarks and brands within this book are for clarifying purposes only and are the owned by the owners themselves, not affiliated with this document.

Introduction

Mothers are considered by many to be the most important person when it comes to parenting. Sometimes it may seem unfair to fathers but that's just the reality in many situations. The instincts of a mother when it comes to her children cannot be underestimated. Even when a child does not say anything, she can easily tell if something is up with the child. A mother is able to discipline a child and show affection even when it is in public. One reason why a mother is sometimes more influential in a child's upbringing is because a mother often spends more time with her children than dads. This is especially true if the dad works out of the home is isn't involved in the child's life at all.

What are the other roles of a mother when it comes to parenting?

The Nurturer

A mother's instinct is usually to be sensitive to her kids. Even a first time women mother can easily pick up what a baby needs when she gives birth to one. The strong emotional bond that a mother and child is sometimes difficult for a father to emulate since the child was in the mother's womb for nine months. It is often a mother's role to look beyond the physical development of a child and look at the changes in behavior and emotions too. Being able to spot this changes allows a mother to deal with the problem even at an early stage so that it does not escalate into a bigger issue.

The Security Anchor

Even when a baby is just a few days old, he can already identify his mother's scent and face. The moment he does, his mother's presence, voice and touch gives him a sense of security. When a child is upset, the typical reaction of a child is to look for mommy. For this reason, a mother must work on strengthening the trust between her and the child. To avoid losing the trust that is already being established then it is important that a mother avoids getting angry without any reason, being impatient, shaming a child in public and even spanking.

This responsibility of a mother is often taken for granted but this is actually just as important because it prevents a child from having any psychological and emotional problems.

The Confidant

It is easy for a mother to talk about problems too with their children because they happen to be more verbal. In general, women tend to talk more than men. Mothers have better listening skills too which is why it is easier for kids to talk to their mothers about their problems. A mother is interested in what is going on with her child even when there is no problem. It's important that mothers learn to keep this communication lines open even when the kids have already grown up. When children get older, they are more likely to turn to their friends so a mother should also be a friend to her kids. A good laugh, frequent interactions and daily interactions are important to maintain this level of friendship with kids.

The Educator

Even when a child has not yet gone to school, a mother has already started the child on many learning activities. A mother has to be patient with the learning pace of a child and to get them started on organizing when they are a little older.

The Disciplinarian

There needs to be a balance between pampering and disciplining a child. Mothers need to be able to teach their kids about responsibility and teach him the important first lessons of life. It's her job to make a child listen and understand to what he has been told. A mother makes a child strong mentally so that he will be ready to face the world when the child goes to school.

And that is for the roles of the mother. But how about us children? What are our duties to our parents? It's not always possible but we should try to do the following:

Honor and respect both our mother and father.
Obey them.
Listen to them.
Take care of them when they are older.
Understand them in times of misunderstandings, failures and breaches.

When we are younger, sometimes it is difficult to understand the things that our parents are trying to make us do and it is difficult to understand their view of things. We feel that they are making us do things that do not represent the real us. But as we get older, we slowly realize why they told us the things that they did and we are slowly starting to understand their actions. When this understanding happens, it is easier to build a relationship with your mother and father.

But is it really important to maintain a good relationship with your mother? The obvious answer to that is yes. It is rare to find a mother who will not go out of her way just to help and protect your children. When you have a strong relationship with your mother, your development process from when you were a baby up to where you are now is going to benefit greatly. You will never feel like you have to face any problems alone because when push comes to shove, you know that your mother will always have your back. When you have a strong bond with your mother, it is easier for you to talk to her about things and ask advice for important matters. There are so many good reasons why you should have a good relationship with your mother. Never underestimate the value of your relationship with your mother.

If you've come to the point where you realize that you do not have a good relationship with her or simply just want to improve whatever relationship you have with her now, you are probably wondering what you can do to make that happen? Well, if you want to find out then you only need to continue reading.

The History of Motherhood

There once was a time when mothers were undervalued and in the era of the Ancient Greek, the idea of motherhood was almost nonexistent. This belief was adapted by the Ancient Romans. They even had images of a patriarch carrying an infant. This particular image failed to recognize the important biological link of a mother to his child. Because of this, the Ancient Romans came up with a law that gave full recognition to the father and he had full authority of the kids that he raised.

From the 11th century up to the 18th century, there was very little change in motherhood. It was considered as something that was inferior although she did get a certain level of autonomy when it comes to caring for the child. After childbirth, it was her responsibility to make decisions for the infant and it was only her that dealt with the child.

Just before the 18th century arrived, there were different models of motherhood that coexisted.

For the working classes, have kids was considered as a necessity and the peasant mothers nurtured their kids. The breastfed their infants and a really specially relationship was created between her and the child. Cuddles and kisses were part of daily life and she did things with her kids. For the upper classes, mothers were expected to have an educational role as they raised their kids to continue whatever legacy and prestige the family had. The role of the mother was lessened though after the Renaissance because children started going to private schools that were created by the church.

For the middle classes, mothers were still close to their children. The often copied the ways of the upper class and sent their children off to school. Some mothers from this class also became nannies of the children from the upper classes. The children of mothers of the lower middle classes were home-schooled.

During the 18th century, motherhood has gained value but they were still given low ranks in the society. The bodies of women which were considered to be the cradle of life received more attention from the doctors. Women or rather maternal love was considered as an important factor in creating a happy society.

Maternal compassion was highly valued because it became the symbol of a nation's solidarity. But despite these improvements, women were still limited to family life. Only the men went to work while women stayed at home to take care of the house and the children.

The 20th century is the time when women slowly distanced themselves from motherhood. They did not just want to be seen as a reproductive organ and some movements even pushed to change the concept of a good mother.

And as you can see today, the roles of mothers have greatly changed. There are so many mothers out there that are now working in different positions while still being able to take care of the kids. Mothers are now looked at as important influences in a child's development.

Section 1: Let Her Know You Love Her

Letting your mother know that you love her might not be the easiest thing to do especially if your mother seems rather cold or distant. But do not let this stop you from letting her know that you love her. Even when she won't respond, the mere fact that she knows you love her will do wonders for your relationship.

There are so many ways to let your mother know that you love her. It's not just limited to telling her repeatedly the words 'I love you'. Did you know that there are five main ways that human beings express their love? They are as follows:

physical touches (hugs, cuddles, kisses)

words of affirmation (compliments, saying I love you)

gifts

acts of service

quality time

The best way for you to let your mother know that you love her is if you express your love to her in the language that she uses instead of your language. Think about it for a while and make some observations. How does she show her love? If you notice that considers quality time as an expression of love then take some time off from your busy life regularly and hang out with her. You guys can cook things together and eat dinner together or whatever activities she is interested in, do it with her. Or is giving gifts her way of showing her affection? If so, give her simple but thoughtful gifts that you know she will enjoy.

When you speak to your mother in the language of love that she is familiar with, then it will be easier for her to understand the message that you are trying to convey. With just one glimpse, she will see right away your intentions are. When you speak to her in her language of love and not yours, you will surely get better and faster results. Letting your mother know that you love her is definitely going to do wonders for your relationship.

Section 2: Let Go Of Emotional Baggage From The Past

You, me, your mother and everyone else around us are not perfect. You have made mistakes in your life. So has she. If you want to be able to improve the relationship that you have with your mother, then it is time for you to start thinking about the past. Stop trying to recall how often she told you were not pretty or not good enough. Yes, this may have caused you a lot of issues in your life. You have probably lost some confidence over the things she said or did and the things she should have done and said. But you're a little older now, surely you understand by now that your mother's words or actions cannot define who you are. Rather, the person you are right now and the person you can be in the future solely depends on the decisions that you make today.

So if you want that relationship with your mother to improve, then it's time to let go of any emotional baggage that you have because of her. You need not forget the things that she has said to you or the things she has done wrong but learn to forgive her for her mistakes and shortcomings. Forgiving and forgetting are two different things. When you do not forgive, you are not allowing yourself to let go of this not so wonderful past. You allow yourself to keep hurting or grieving for it. When you are still hurt, it is hard for your relationship to progress into something better. So forgive your mother for whatever she has done wrong.

Yes, forgiving does not come easy for everyone especially if the wound is quite deep. But then again ask yourself, what do you have to gain if you keep holding onto that anger or resentment? Nothing but negative feelings. If it makes you feel any better, you can discuss this with your mother so you can let it all out in the open and maybe even get her side of things. Maybe getting her side of the story might be all you need to better understand the past and why it happened.

Maybe that's all you need to be able to forgive her. In the end, you have nothing but good things to gain from forgiving your mother for whatever is that is causing a rift between the two of you. You are setting yourself free from such a heavy burden and you are now at a point where creating a better relationship with your mother is entirely possible. And it is one less thing to stress about.

Section 3: Be Patient

So you've decided to start changing the way you act towards your mother so that you and her can have a better relationship. After doing a few things, you start getting discouraged because nothing seems to be working. In fact, the only thing you seem to be getting are negative reactions like being pushed away or her getting upset.

As you can see, improving your relationship with your mother is not something that happens overnight. Doing a few nice things is not enough to undo the years and years of problems, misunderstanding, fights and so on. When you make the decision to improve your relationship with your mother, you need to be realistic with your expectations and your efforts. This is a journey that will take years and months. It is not something with a step by step guide wherein you can see the results in a matter of weeks or months.

Say for example, as you were growing up you became the rebellious one or maybe somebody who disobeyed them whenever possible. And now put yourselves in her shoes. The child who disobeyed almost everything that you said is now suddenly acting like the nicest person on the planet. What would you think? You'd wonder why, right?

Don't take it against your mom. But as you can see, you have spent so many years being the old you. There might have been times in the past when you promised her that you would change or be better. Maybe you managed to do it for a while but just went back to your old ways eventually. Maybe your mom is thinking that this is one of those times again. And can you really blame her? After all the hurt that you have caused her, she has probably put up walls and hardened herself so that you cannot hurt her again or she won't get disappointed anymore.

If you really want to improve the relationship that you have with your mom then you need to be patient. Since you will not see results right away, you need to continue with your efforts. The change won't be instantaneous either. She won't wake up one day forgetting about everything and suddenly you and her are hitting it off so well. Little by little your mother will start warming up to you after your consistent efforts. You need to have patience in convincing her that you have really changed this time and the change is for good. You need to be patient as she slowly allows herself to be convinced by your consistent actions.

Section 4: Drop The Ideal Parent-Child Relationship

Don't we all have an idea of an ideal relationship when it comes to relationships? Even with how our relationship with our parents should go, we also have a picture in our mind of how it should be. You might have probably gotten this ideal while watching TV or seeing the interaction between your friends and their mothers.

However, for your relationship with your mom to blossom, you need to let go of whatever ideal you have created in your mind. This ideal is preventing the relationship to grow. Let go of it. The sooner, the better. Stop wishing for your mom to be like your best friend or somebody you can talk to about anything and everything under the sun. Someone that you can do things with and all that stuff. Stop expecting your mother to not hold back when showing her affection to you. Again, drop whatever ideal that you have because it is not helping your relationship with her at all.

Why? When you work on improving a relationship with a certain ideal in mind, you are setting expectations that may not be a reality. You are asking your mother to be someone that she is not. When you force her to start having these conversations where you should talk about anything and everything, you will only get resistance from her. You will start getting frustrated and it might make you give up on your efforts to improve the relationship with your mother.

When you drop the ideal that you have, you might even be surprised to see that your mother is actually trying to reach out to you. You prevent your relationship with her from blossoming into something wonderful. Expecting a relationship to grow in a certain way is definitely not the way.

You are probably being unfair about this too because it is most likely that this ideal that you have in your mind is not something that you consulted her about. It may be ideal to you but it not might be ideal for your mother. The only time an ideal should be set in place is if you and your mother have had a decision about it and have both agreed to this ideal.

If you have not, then let the ideal go and allow your relationship with your mother to grow by giving her space to grow too. Stop expecting your mother to be something and stop being so fixated on this ideal in your mind. Let that go!

Section 5: Appreciate What They Have To Offer

You want your mother to be able to talk to you about everything. You do not want her to hold back. Or maybe you want your mother to be a certain kind of person. You want her to be more open to the suggestions that you are making. You want her to stop resisting everything that you have ever wanted to do. Or how about being more fashionable? When our mother is unable to meet what we want her to be, we get frustrated.

But maybe you should stop doing that. Again, this goes back to letting go of whatever ideals you have in your mind. What you should do instead is learn to appreciate what your mom can give and what she is capable of.

So let us take a look at this example. You want your mother to come with you on a shopping trip or maybe even just dining out somewhere. Your mother makes it. However, it is not good enough for you because it is only once a month. You think that it is ideal for you and your mom to bond at least once a week. And no matter how often you arrange for you and your mom to see each other, it only happens once a month. Frustrating right? Well it does not have to be if you learn to let go of your ideal. Appreciate the fact instead that despite her business or maybe physical difficulties to go out, she still manages to see you once a month. When you do this, you will be creating a smoother relationship for you two because there will be much lesser friction.

Do not get frustrated when your mom clams up every time you ask her about something. Maybe it is not like her to be talkative and things that she shares are selected. When you impose your want or need on your mom, you are only being selfish. Drop this selfishness. Think of the things that you know your mom likes to do and find some way for you to incorporate that in your life so that she will feel that even though you are all grown up now, she still has room in your life. If you know that your mom enjoys cooking then instead of eating out when you are home then don't eat out often. Instead, let her cook and maybe help her out instead so that you can have some time to bond while waiting for the food to be served.

Section 6: Look Beneath The Ideals

And yes, we are back to ideals again. The ideal of a mother-child relationship that we have is our mind's way of visualizing something that we want. When we have an ideal, it represents a need that we want to be fulfilled. If you will be able to tackle the reason why you have this particular ideal, then the sooner you will be able to deal with your need. Fulfilling an ideal and fulfilling a need can be two different things.

Take a look at this example. A daughter is wishing that mother would be a better mentor figure. But since the mother is always preoccupied with other things, she thinks that her mother is not fulfilling that and she lacks a mother figure. As a result, she turned to others for a mother figure and to get some guidance. Even though she already has the guidance that she needs, she still wishes for her mother to take on the role of being a mentor.

Apparently, the daughter was not lacking any guidance. In fact, she has more than enough of it. But when you take a look beyond the surface or the ideal, you realize that the reason she wanted her mother to be her mentor is because that was how she perceived love. Loving to her meant watching over the person that you love, showing you care and so on. She did not perceive her mother's other efforts as a way of showing love.

So take a look at yourself and the ideal that you have. Why do you have that ideal? When you meet your ideal, will your need also be fulfilled?
Sometimes your mother might not reciprocate your actions but it does not mean that she does not love you. Maybe your language of love is different from one another. If you learn her way of expressing their love, then you will clearly see that she has made efforts to show you that she loves you but you just did not see it. Because once again, you were to hung up on the ideal that you had.

You may be looking at the wrong places. Your mother has her way of showing you that she loves her. She is probably busy with her work because she wants financial stability. Financial stability means a family is being taken care of.

So there goes another reason why we should let go of our ideals. Getting our ideals do not really mean anything but just images that we make up in our mind. Do not judge your mother's love for you based on her capability to meet the ideals that you have set for her.

Section 7: Start With Channels That Are Existing And Open

If your relationship with your mother is quite sour, then you might want to begin with whatever channel is still open between you two. What are the methods that you two stay in touch? Do you have a fixed monthly dinner? Do you randomly call each other? Do you send text messages? That is where you should begin and then just start climbing the ladder from there.

So take a look at this example. During the time when your relationship with your mother started going sour, you started have numerous arguments, you slammed doors in front of her while still engaged in a verbal fight or maybe there was too much shouting. This could have closed so many doors for both of you. Now that you are trying to improve your relationship with your mom, you are getting a lot of resistance every time you try to get a conversation going. Apparently, having conversations is one of the closed channels because of all the yelling and arguments in the past.

So what should you do? What are the things that your mother usually ask help from you from? Or what things does she still do for you? If your mom frequently asks you what you want to have for breakfast, lunch and dinner then take the opportunity to leave your meals in her more than capable hands. Instead of dining out frequently or telling your mom that you do not mind and you will just eat outside, let her do this for you.

If your mother likes to watch TV series, then sit and watch it with her even if you do not really like whatever it is that you are watching. Even though conversations are off-limits at the moment, you can spend time with your mother instead.

Once you are able to settle comfortably in the channels that are available to both of you, you can slowly add another layer so that you can continue building your relationship. When your mother is preparing your meals, there is an opportunity for you two to talk since your mom will need to ask you what you want to eat. And from there, you can slowly start talking about other things which means you are slowly opening the channel for you to talk.

Be receptive also to your mother's language of love. If she wants to take you to the airport, then allow her to do so even if you think it is only going to be a waste of her time. This is her way of letting you see that she loves you so accept the offer.

No matter how bad your relationship might be with your mother, there must be something that you can start with. If you cannot really find anything like you do not have any contact with your mom anymore, try using the last communication mode that you two had before everything went bad.

Section 8: Avoid Asking For Advice Unless You Really Want It

Sometimes we are only seeking for the approval of our parents when we ask them for their opinion or their advice. But you need to remember that you are no longer the little kid that you used to be. You are all grown up now. This means that you are old enough to make decisions on your own. You do not need to ask your mother about which color to paint your living room or if you should get your own car, unless of course you are truly seeking her advice. If your mother approves of something that you do or a decision that you have made, she will let you know. It might not be in a way that you expect because she will likely give you her approval in a way that she is comfortable with.

However, if your mother is really fixated on giving you advise, do not tell her to shut up either. Be polite and listen to what she says. If it's something that you do not agree on at all, gently let her know. Otherwise, just smile and nod. But do not let her words go right through the other ear. Listen to it because who know, you might find helpful when you have had the chance to think about it more.

When your mother gives you her opinion or an advice, it is not because she wants to be selfish or anything bad. You need to remember that your mother is only trying let you know what she feels is the best for you and what she thinks is best for you. After you've thought about what she has said, do not be afraid to make a choice. Do not feel guilty when you do not follow what she said.

Section 9: Solve Your Own Personal Or Financial Issues

Again, you are all grown up now. It is time you learn to stand up on your own feet and stop relying on the resources that she has. Your mother will not be able to work forever and she will need to save up for her retirement too. If you have issues with your partner, do not ask your mother to settle it for you either. Of course you can ask her for advice but don't rely on her to fix your issues with other people. If there is anything that you can depend on your mother for, it is her emotional support.

When you need somebody to listen to you as you pour your heart out or vent out your feelings, then that should be okay. If you need someone to help you organize the jumbled thoughts that you have, let her give you a hand. But don't, and I mean never, ask her to resolve things for you.

Why? Like I said, you are not a kid anymore. You are more than capable of resolving your issues even when it feels like you cannot do it. No matter how big or small a problem is, there will be a solution for it. You just need to be persistent in finding out what that solution is.

Besides, being able to resolve your own problem especially the big ones will give your confidence and self-esteem a good boost. And of course, you are making your mother proud of you. Despite the rough seas, you still managed to make it back to the shore.

Conclusion

Do not ever think that the relationship that you have with your mother cannot be fixed anymore. No matter how bad the situation is right now between the two of you, there is always a way to make it better. Like they say, you should never lose hope especially in things that you truly want and believe in. You just need to trust yourself. You need to have faith that it will be better one day. But of course, do not expect that it will change without you doing anything.

If you want your relationship with your mother to improve, do not expect that it will change with just a few nice deeds especially if your relationship has been severely damaged over the past years. If you want to improve your relationship with her, you need to make an effort. The efforts that you make should not be sporadic. Rather, you should remain consistent in your actions.

You do not want your mom thinking that this is something temporary. Learn to be patient because the changes won't happen overnight either. But if you stay consistent with your efforts, you will eventually see changes or improvements in your relationship with your mother.

There are actually so many ways that you can do to improve your relationship with your mother. If you want her to know that you love her, express it in a way that she can easily understand. This means that you should not enforce your language of love but rather be open to her language of love.

And stop having ideals. Ideals are bad in a way because they prevent your relationship with your mother to grow as it should be. You are forcing it to be something it isn't. Instead of being so fixated on the ideal, drop it and open your eyes. You will eventually see that what you have been looking for has always been there. You just failed to see it because you were too set on making your ideal mother-child relationship a reality.

Again, there is no mother-child relationship that cannot be fixed as long as efforts are being exerted to improve the relationship. Do not wait before it is too late. Start improving your relationship with your mother now and you'll be surprised at how wonderful it will feel to have a better relationship with your mom.

EXPERIENCE
EVERYTHING
P U B L I S H I N G

www.ingramcontent.com/pod-product-compliance
Lightning Source LLC
Chambersburg PA
CBHW071809020426
42331CB00008B/2449